7000438

CONTENTS

KEY POINTS

- The main objectives of an appraisal system are usually to review employees' performance and potential. There may also be a link with a reward review.

- Appraisals can benefit both employers and employees by improving job performance, by making it easier to identify strengths and weaknesses and by determining suitability for development.

- In designing a scheme it is necessary to decide who should be appraised; who does the appraising; how often appraisals take place and whether employees should see their appraisal reports.

- Employers are not required by law to introduce appraisal schemes. There are however some aspects of employment legislation that affect employee appraisal.

What are <u>appraisals</u>?

Appraisals regularly record an assessment of an employee's performance, potential and development needs. The appraisal is an opportunity to take an overall view of work content, loads and volume, to look back on what has been achieved during the reporting period and agree objectives for the next.

What are the <u>objectives of appraisals</u>?

The objectives of the appraisal scheme should be determined before the system is designed in detail. The objectives will to a large extent <u>dictate the methods and performance criteria</u> for appraisal so they should be <u>discussed with employees, managers and trade unions</u> to obtain their views and commitment. The main objectives of an appraisal system are usually to <u>review performance</u>, <u>potential</u> and <u>identify training and career planning needs</u>. In addition the appraisal system may be used to determine whether employees should receive an element of <u>financial reward</u> for their performance.

* **<u>Performance reviews</u>** – give managers and employees opportunities to discuss how employees are progressing and to see what sort of improvements can be made or help given to build on their strengths and enable them to perform more effectively.

* **<u>Review of potential and development needs</u>** – predicts the <u>level</u> and <u>type of work</u> that employees will be capable of doing <u>in the future</u> and how they can be best developed for the sake of their own career and to maximise their contribution to the organisation.

* **<u>Reward reviews</u>** – determine the 'rewards' that employees will get for their past work. The reward review is usually a separate process from the appraisal system but the review is often assisted by information provided by the performance appraisal.

What are the <u>benefits of appraisals</u>?

Appraisals can help to improve employees' job performance by <u>identifying</u> strengths and weaknesses and determining how their strengths can be best utilised within the organisation and weaknesses overcome. They can help to reveal problems which may be restricting employees' progress and causing inefficient work practices.

3

Some employers may talk to their employees regularly about their problems and performance at work and may not therefore see the need for a formal appraisal system. Regular dialogue between managers and their staff about work performance should of course be encouraged. However, in the absence of a formal appraisal scheme much will depend on the attitude of individual managers. Some will give regular feedback on their employees' performance and potential whilst others will neglect this responsibility. An appraisal system can develop a greater degree of consistency by ensuring that managers and employees meet formally and regularly to discuss performance and potential. Experience shows this can encourage better performance from employees.

Appraisals can also provide information for manpower planning to assist succession planning and to determine the suitability of employees for promotion, for particular types of employment and training. In addition they can improve communications by giving employees an opportunity to talk about their ideas and expectations and to be told how they are progressing. This process can also improve the quality of working life by increasing mutual understanding between managers and employees.

Is a formal appraisal system suitable for smaller companies?

Smaller companies can certainly benefit from having appropriate appraisal systems. Indeed, the task of appraising employees is usually easier because managers are more likely to know each employee well. It is important however that the appraisal system is designed to meet the particular needs of the smaller company and is not over elaborate. An appraisal system does not need to generate a lot of paper to be effective; on the contrary the most effective systems are often the simplest. ACAS can help organisations of all sizes to devise and introduce systems which meet their particular needs.

No organisation, whether large or small, should contemplate the introduction of a formal appraisal system unless it is fully committed to its success and clear about its objectives. A scheme will involve the investment of time and money. Managers will need to be trained to carry out appraisal properly; employees will need to be fully and carefully informed about how it will affect them. A badly designed appraisal system operated by untrained and poorly motivated managers and hastily introduced will damage relationships and provide no benefits.

Who should be appraised?

In the past most appraisals have been carried out for 'white collar' employees. However this helps to perpetuate the feeling of 'them and us'. The appraisal of 'blue collar' employees can improve their motivation and can help them to make useful suggestions about how their jobs can operate more effectively. In addition growing interest in flexible working practices, the harmonisation of terms and conditions of employment and the growth of new technology have blurred the differences between 'blue' and 'white collar' workers[1] and many organisations are now extending the benefits of appraisal to all employees. Appendix 3 gives an example of an appraisal form which has been devised for manual employees.

Who should carry out the appraisal?

In most organisations employees are appraised by their immediate managers on the grounds that those who delegate work and monitor performance are best placed to appraise performance. Others argue that appraisals carried out at a more senior level allow employees an opportunity to talk with higher management who, in turn, can find out the views and attitudes of more junior staff at first hand.

Perhaps the best approach is for employees' immediate superiors to write and carry out appraisals and for more senior managers to have an opportunity to comment on the report. This enables senior managers to keep a regular check on the progress of staff and to monitor the appraisal system to ensure that reporting standards are consistent.

How often should appraisals take place?

Employee appraisal should be a continuous process and should not be limited to a formal review once a year. The frequency of formal appraisals will depend on the nature of the organisation and on the objectives of the system. For example, in a high technology organisation objectives may be changing quickly so that formal appraisals may need to be carried out more than once a year. In an environment which is less subject to change, annual appraisals may be sufficient. Most employees receive a formal appraisal annually,

---

[1] See ACAS Discussion Paper No 1 *Harmonisation*.

although more frequent appraisals are often needed for new employees, for longer serving staff who have moved to new posts or for those who are below acceptable performance standards.

Should employees see their appraisal reports?

It is sensible to allow employees to see at least some parts of their appraisal reports. Where reports are only partially open it is usually the section on potential/ promotion prospects which is not disclosed. If reporting is 'open' employees should have the opportunity to sign the completed form and to express their views on the appraisal they have received; in particular whether they feel it is a fair assessment of their work over the reporting period.

It is sometimes argued that 'open reporting' discourages managers from giving candid appraisals of staff. In order to avoid conflict managers may not accurately convey some of the more critical comments they have written on the report. However, if employees are unable to see their reports they will not know whether the verbal feedback accurately reflects what was put on the report by the manager or the areas where improvement is required. In practice managers are more likely to make fair and accurate comments on

'Employees may not know whether the verbal feedback accurately reflects what was put on the report by the manager.'

the appraisal form if they are aware that the form will be shown to the employee and that they will have to substantiate their written comments at the appraisal interview. Where managers have a tendency to be too generous in an open reporting system, this can be counteracted by training, monitoring and by allowing more senior managers to comment on the reports.

What are the legal considerations?

There is no legal obligation on employers to introduce appraisal systems. However, organisations need to be aware of some aspects of employment legislation that affect employee appraisal. An outline of the legal considerations is contained in Appendix 1.

MAKING A SUCCESS OF APPRAISALS

KEY POINTS

For appraisal schemes to work effectively it is necessary to:

- Make sure that senior managers are fully committed to the idea of appraisals.

- Consult with managers, employees and trade union representatives about the design and implementation of appraisals before they are introduced.

- Monitor schemes regularly.

- Give appraisers adequate training to enable them to make fair and objective assessments and to carry out effective appraisal interviews.

- Keep the scheme as simple and straightforward as possible.

A Checklist

Senior managers must be committed to the idea of appraisals. They should fully accept that those who carry out the appraisals will need to be properly trained and have sufficient time and resources available to complete interviews, fill in the forms and carry out follow up work.

Consult with managers, employees and trade union representatives before appraisals are introduced. They should be consulted, and agreement sought about the objectives and the appraisal methods. A pilot scheme should then be developed and tested amongst a representative sample of managers and employees. Appendix 2 contains a checklist of items which need to be considered before an appraisal system is introduced.

Make the scheme as straightforward as possible. Appraisal systems can sometimes fail because of over-elaborate paper work. It is essential to design the recording systems for those who will be using them and to keep any forms as simple and as clearly written as possible.

A timetable should be fixed for the implementation of the scheme. All employees and trade union representatives should be provided with written information describing how appraisal will work and how it will affect them. New employees will need to be fully informed about the appraisal system as part of their induction. All employees should be briefed and told in writing about the overall objectives of the scheme, how the appraisal system will work and what is expected of them individually. It is useful to nominate someone to answer employees' queries – either directly or through their union representative.

Provide adequate training. All managers who carry out appraisals must receive training to help them assess performance effectively and to put that skill into use in the appraisal process. Appraisers should receive written instructions on how to complete reports and they should also be given the opportunity to practise these skills and to receive feedback on their performance. It is a useful training exercise for managers to write employee appraisal reports which are based on case studies. They should then be given the opportunity to discuss their appraisal reports with others in the training group and to discuss any differences in markings. Trainees should also be allowed to practice 'mock' appraisal interviews and to receive constructive comments on their performance from tutors and from others in the group.

Make sure that managers carry out appraisals. Some appraisal schemes fail simply because managers give low priority to appraisals. A senior manager should therefore be given responsibility for co-ordinating the scheme and for ensuring that

'Trainees should be allowed to practice mock appraisal interviews.'

interviews are held and that the forms are completed correctly. The appraisal of managers' own performance can usefully include consideration of how effectively they undertake appraisals. Some organisations set an annual timetable for the completion of various stages of the appraisal process and circulate this timetable to all appraisers. Another method is to spread appraisals throughout the year, possibly on the anniversary of the employee's appointment. This takes the pressure off the line manager to carry out a large number of appraisals at the same time.

Monitor the appraisal system. Check that appraisals are being carried out properly and determine whether the system needs to be modified to meet the changing needs of the organisation. The views of managers should be obtained about the scheme in general and in relation to any problems they have encountered. It is also important to get reactions from employees and trade union representatives

10

concerning their experiences on being appraised. The formal appraisal system should be updated regularly. Schemes will become ineffective if they are not modified to take account of changes in the size of the organisation, in products, skills and occupational groupings or arising from the introduction of new technology.

KEY POINTS

- It is essential to have written records of the appraisal to provide a feedback to employees and to allow more senior managers to monitor the effectiveness of appraisals.

- The job description helps to focus attention on the employee's performance at work and to avoid assessing character.

- SOME APPRAISAL TECHNIQUES:

  Rating – A number of employee characteristics are rated on a scale which may range from 'outstanding' to 'unacceptable'.

  Comparison with objectives – Employees and their managers agree objectives. The appraisal is based on how far these objectives have been met.

  Critical Incidents – The appraiser records incidents of employees' positive and negative behaviour during a given period.

  Narrative report – The appraiser describes the individual's work performance in his or her own words.

  Behaviourally anchored rating scales – A group of rating scales are developed which are custom made for each job.

- It is important to set up a procedure for employees to appeal against their assessment.

Paperwork is not an end in itself but it is essential to have written records of the appraisal to provide a feedback to employees and to allow more senior managers to monitor the effectiveness of appraisals. The design of forms will depend on the nature of the organisation, the objectives of the system and the employees to be appraised. However, most performance appraisal forms should contain provision for:

- basic personal details, ie. name, department, post, length of time in the job
- job title
- job description
- a detailed review of the individual's performance against a set of job related criteria
- an overall performance rating
- general comments by a more senior manager
- comments by the employee
- a plan for development and action.

In addition there should be some guidance notes explaining the objectives of the scheme and how the appraisal interview should be conducted.

What is the purpose of the job description?

A job title and a brief description of the main objectives and duties of the job should feature at the beginning of the employee appraisal form. The job description should be agreed between the manager and the employee and should estimate the percentage of time taken up with each of the duties. The job description should help appraisers to focus attention on the employee's performance at work and to avoid assessing character. An example of a job description is given in Appendix 4.

What are the different methods of performance appraisal?

Rating

This method lists a number of factors to be assessed such as quality and output of work, which are then rated on a numerical scale according to level of performance, for example:

1 outstanding
2 exceeds requirements of the job
3 meets the requirements of the job
4 shows some minor weaknesses

5   shows some significant weaknesses

6   unacceptable.

The rating scales method is easy to construct, use and understand. However, it is highly subjective, there is often a tendency to bunch the ratings around the average point and an overall impression can infleunce all the individual assessments. An example of a rating scales appraisal is given in Appendix 4.

Comparison with objectives

Under this system, the employee and his or her manager agree objectives at the beginning of the appraisal period. The subsequent appraisal is based on how far these objectives have been met.

This method is more objective than rating scales because the emphasis is on work achievement. It can be more participative because it gives employees the chance to agree their objectives and enables them to carry out a form of self appraisal. On the debit side there may be some employees who do not welcome the element of self direction – because they would rather be told what to do.

An important consideration in using this system is whether changes in circumstances which are beyond the individual's control, such as the economic environment, can result in objectives becoming unrealistic. It is therefore wise to take stock, perhaps mid-way through a reporting period, and decide whether there is a need to revise objectives because of unforeseen circumstances. An example of a comparison with objectives appraisal form is given in Appendix 5.

It is worth stressing that rating scales used alone do not always take full account of results, while the objectives method can lack analysis of performance. Some organisations therefore combine the two methods in their appraisal system.

Critical incidents

Using this method the appraiser is required to record incidents of employees' positive and negative behaviour during a given period. The appraiser is expected to give feedback on this behaviour when it occurs whether it be to show appreciation of good performance or to give counselling to help poor performance. The record of incidents throughout the year forms the basis of the appraisal report.

This method of appraisal encourages frequent recording and enables employees' performance to be judged on actual incidents rather than on subjective assessments. It also helps to overcome the problem of annual reporting which can concentrate unduly on events immediately prior to the appraisal.

The critical incident method can however be time consuming and burdensome and it can result in overactive supervision; some employees may feel that everything they do is being observed and recorded. In addition it may be an inappropriate method of appraisal in jobs where there is little opportunity to show initiative. The critical incidents method is sometimes used to supplement other techniques.

Narrative report

This technique requires the appraiser to describe the individual's work performance and behaviour in his or her own words. The narrative report may take the form of an essay or a controlled written report, such as answers to certain headings or guidelines. This approach is sometimes combined with rating scales. Narrative reporting is flexible and can enable the appraiser to gear the report to specific circumstances. However, its effectiveness depends largely on the literary ability of the appraiser. It is also difficult to make comparison between employees because entirely different factors may be assessed by different appraisers.

'The effectiveness of narrative reporting depends largely on the literary ability of the appraiser.'

Behaviourally Anchored Rating Scales (BARS)

This is a comparatively new method which overcomes some of the problems with conventional rating scales.

- Meetings are held with the managers who will rate the people holding the job in question. These managers are then asked to list several key aspects of performance in the particular job. For example, for a departmental retail store manager a rating scale could include 'handling customer complaints' and 'meeting day to day deadlines'.

- The same or a different group provides examples of good, average and poor performance for each category. For a retail store manager's category in relation to deadlines, an example of very good behaviour would be 'Could be expected never to be late in meeting deadlines, no matter how unusual the circumstances'. An example of poor behaviour would be 'Could be expected to disregard due dates in ordering and run out of a major line in his or her department'.

- A number of such categories or 'anchors' is generated and each is given a value ranging perhaps from 1 (very poor behaviour) to 7 (outstanding behaviour). The number of categories to be rated will vary according to the nature of the job but most schemes have between 6 and 9.

- Once the scheme is completed appraisers use it to evaluate the expected behaviour of each person being rated. Individual rating scales are constructed on the basis of each job holder's typical or expected behaviour on each scale.

The advantage of BARS is that the anchor scales are directly applicable to the job being evaluated and are therefore more precise than the often vague traits used in conventional rating scales. On the other hand it is costly and time consuming to introduce.

36_2

Appeals

In order to preserve the credibility of the appraisal scheme it is necessary to set up a procedure for employees to appeal against their assessment. This may be through a special procedure linked to the appraisal system or through the grievance procedure. The procedure should provide for the employee to be assisted by a union representative or a representative of his or her choice. Appeals should be made to a more senior manager than the appraiser. In some organisations appeals are made to a committee consisting of management and union representatives. The appeals procedure should be used only in exceptional circumstances. The main aim of appraisals is to help employees improve their performance. The appraisal system should not be used to discipline poor performers nor as a device for employees to negotiate better markings or performance payments through the appeals procedure. Frequent use of the appeals procedure could indicate that there are problems with the appraisal system and a need for further management training in appraisal techniques.

KEY POINTS

- Some of the inconsistencies associated with performance appraisal can be overcome if senior managers have an opportunity to comment upon and sign the appraisal.

- A manager should be nominated to monitor and co-ordinate the appraisal system.

- Managers should keep running records on the performance of their staff throughout the reporting period.

- Suitable training will help to achieve consistency in reporting standards.

The 'halo' or 'horns' effect

In some cases appraisers may allow the rating they give to one characteristic to excessively influence their ratings on all subsequent factors. The appraiser who decides that the employee is good in one important aspect and gives him or her similarly high markings for all other aspects is demonstrating the 'halo' effect. Alternatively one serious fault can sometimes lead an appraiser to reduce markings in other areas (the 'horns' effect).

This problem can be resolved if the appraiser judges all employees on a single factor or trait before going on to the next factor. In this way it is possible to consider all employees relative to a standard or to each other on each factor.

'One serious fault can sometimes lead an appraiser to reduce markings in other areas (the 'horns' effect).'

Variations in reporting standards

Some appraisers are either over generous or too critical in their markings. Reporting standards can be evened out if senior managers have an opportunity to confirm the markings, make further comments and sign the appraisal, thereby enabling them to compare reporting standards and to identify and counsel any managers who appear to be too generous or too harsh in their reporting.

The manager nominated to monitor the appraisal system should also seek to identify any variations in reporting standards and offer help to those managers who need it.

Emphasis on the recent past

Most appraisals report on a period of one year. Some managers, when completing reports, may find it difficult to recall and assess events that occurred in the earlier part of the reporting year. The lapse of time tends to encourage an emphasis on more recent events, which can distort the balance of the report.

This problem can be resolved if managers keep running records on the performance of their staff and of actual events which are evidence of work performance. These notes will provide a very valuable *aide memoire* when the time comes for the reports themselves to be written. Alternatively managers may wish to make an informal record half way through the reporting period to help them be objective in the end of year assessment.

The central tendency

Some appraisers are reluctant to rate people at the outer ends of the rating scale, especially if the rating system has an odd number of rating points when there may be a tendency to mark employees in the middle scale. Rating systems which have an even number of scales (and therefore no 'middle scale') have the merit of requiring raters to mark above or below the 'middle line'.

Suitable training will help to achieve consistency in reporting standards. There should also be guidance provided on the report form, which should contain an explanation of the requirements of each part of the report.

KEY POINTS

Appraisal of employees' potential can be based on:

- past performance and observations from senior managers
- employees' assessment of their own potential and performance
- reports from assessment centres.

'Employees' assessment of their own performance and potential is important although highly subjective.'

It is not always easy to assess employees' potential for different kinds and levels of work because the predictions are usually based on past performance, and jobs at higher levels may have different performance demands. However, it is necessary to assess potential in order to determine how employees' aptitudes can be best utilised in the organisation and to identify those who appear suitable for further training and promotion.

Past performance

Reports from employees' immediate managers and observations from more senior managers are an important although incomplete way of identifying potential. Managers may have observed the individual only in a narrow range of tasks, which may not necessarily be an indication of suitability for higher level work. Whether someone has failed or been successful in a lower level job is relevant but not necessarily crucial to the assessment of his or her potential.

A section for reviewing potential sometimes appears on the performance appraisal document. It is however preferable to provide a specially designed form, or at least a separate section, with separate instructions on how it is to be completed. An example of a form for assessing potential is given in Appendix 6.

Self assessment

Employees' assessment of their own performance and potential is important, although highly subjective. During appraisal interviews managers should attempt to find out whether employees are interested in different kinds of work; where practicable this should be followed by plans to realise this potential through training courses, assignments and planned experience.

Assessment centres

There has been an increase in the use of centres for assessing the potential of staff. Assessment centres are used by a number of companies and staffed by trained assessors, usually psychologists, who use a variety of group and individual psychometric tests in assessing employees' potential.

Assessment centres have an advantage in that they are more objective than other methods of evaluating the potential of employees. However, they are relatively expensive and time consuming.

23

363

KEY POINTS

- Employees should be given adequate notice of the appraisal interview. Self assessment forms can help them prepare.

- At least one hour should be set aside for the interview.

- Seating arrangements should be comfortable and the interview free from interruptions.

- The appraiser should suggest ways in which the employee's good work can be continued and how he or she can achieve further improvement.

- Both parties should discuss how far agreed objectives have been met and agree future objectives.

Preparing for the interview

Employees should be given adequate notice of appraisal interviews. Self assessment forms completed by employees before their interviews can help them note what they think have been their strong and weak points; what they see as barriers to effective performance; their plans for the coming year and their development and training needs. Self assessment forms are an *aide memoire* to the individual and they do not have to be shown to the person conducting the appraisal. An example of a self assessment form is given in Appendix 7.

The manager should consider the overall results attained by the employee and, where the results have been significantly greater or lower than expected, possible reasons for variations in performance. This will be easier if notes have been made throughout the year of the employee's successes and failures, and any performance related developments beyond the employee's control.

At least one hour should be set aside for the interview. The seating should be comfortable and arranged to create an informal atmosphere. The interview should be free from interruptions.

'The seating arrangement should be comfortable, and arranged to create an informal atmosphere.'

The structure of the interview

The interviewer should:

- explain the purpose and scope of the interview
- discuss the job in terms of its objectives and demands
- encourage the employee to discuss his or her strengths and weaknesses

- discuss how far agreed objectives have been met
- agree future objectives
- discuss any development needs appropriate to the existing job or the individual's future in the organisation eg. training, education, work experience
- summarise the plans which are agreed
- if there are disagreements explain how the employee can appeal against his or her appraisal markings.

During the interview

It is essential to ask questions that draw out the employee's reactions and ideas. Leading questions or questions which only require a 'yes' or 'no' response should be avoided.

Managers should put employees at ease by beginning their interviews with fairly casual, routine remarks. It is preferable to discuss employees' strong points first and to place emphasis on good work already done. Employees should be encouraged to suggest ways in which their good work can be continued and their views sought on how they can achieve further improvement. Another way to start the interview is for managers to ask employees what successes they feel they have achieved during the past year and which things they are least pleased with.

If it is necessary to improve performance it will be counter productive to gloss over employees' weak points and stress their good features in order to make the interview as friendly as possible. It is important to encourage employees to discuss their weaknesses openly and to encourage them to suggest ways in which they can improve. Interviewers should not impose their own solutions. These should emerge as a result of joint discussion.

After the interview

Shortly after the interview the manager should summarise in writing the main points of the discussion and the action which was agreed, and give a copy to the employee. If the appraisal scheme is to have credibility, it is essential that managers follow up any points arising from the interview and carry out any agreed action. For example, it may be necessary to organise training or help to overcome any obstacles to the employee's effectiveness which were mentioned at the interview.

KEY POINTS

- Reward reviews provide for salary increments, bonuses and similar incentives to be awarded on the basis of an employee's performance.

- There is usually a link with the appraisal system but the reward review should take place at a different time from the appraisal interview.

- Employers should carefully examine their existing pay, benefits and appraisal systems before they decide to introduce reward reviews.

- Consultation should take place with managers, employees and trade unions, and agreement reached before such schemes are introduced.

Performance appraisal systems alone can motivate, improve performance and create greater job satisfaction without the inducement of additional reward. However, there is increasing interest in reward reviews and the links with performance assessment.

What are reward reviews?

Under this system salary increments, bonuses and similar incentives are awarded on the basis of an employee's performance. For example, merit pay is a payment system where the employee receives a bonus or level of basic pay linked to a systematic assessment of his or her performance or conduct.[2]

What are the pros and cons of reward reviews?

Reward reviews can be a cost effective method of motivating employees by providing cash incentives to effective performers. They can also provide incentives to those employees whose work is not easily measurable. However, the assessments on which rewards are based are usually subjective. Reward reviews can also be divisive because employees who do not receive payments may complain of favouritism and may eventually become discouraged.

'The appraisal interview is likely to be more constructive when pay is not part of the discussion.'

What is the link between performance assessment and reward reviews?

The reward review is usually a separate process from the appraisal system but is often based on some of the information provided by the performance appraisal. Most organisations carry out the appraisal review at a separate time from the reward review. The appraisal interview is likely to be more constructive when pay is not part of the discussion because the disclosure of the salary review figure is likely to obscure a genuine discussion both of achievements and of areas where improvement is necessary.

How can reward reviews be made to work successfully?

Employers should carefully examine their existing pay, benefits and appraisal systems before they decide whether to introduce reward reviews. Such schemes will probably fail if they are introduced quickly with the aim of shoring up ineffective payments systems or inadequate levels of pay. Conversely, a poor or inappropriate appraisal and rewards scheme can distort or otherwise damage an effective pay system, create deep dissatisfactions and demotivate.

Organisations should ensure that:

- consultation takes place with managers, employees and trade unions, and agreement reached before the scheme is introduced
- systems are relatively simple to understand, operate and monitor
- managers are properly trained and have sufficient time available to carry out the reviews
- managers, employees and their representatives are given clear information on how reward reviews will operate
- the appraisal system is kept separate from the reward review procedure
- the system is closely monitored by more senior managers
- employees have an opportunity to see and to make comments on their assessment markings
- an appeals procedure is available.

What are the types of reward review?

There are considerable variations in the types of reward review. Although some organisations have replaced annual increments with merit only increases, the most common practice is for a reward payment to supplement 'across the board' increases.

Some examples of reward reviews are:

- Fixed incremental scales with limited flexibility. The manager/supervisor agrees the pay increase for the majority of his or her staff but can increase payments for exceptionally effective staff or reduce the payment for poor performers.

- Performance pay linked to an incremental scale. Attainment of the next point on the scale is dependent on the employee reaching a satisfactory performance rating.

- Pay increases based on performance ratings and awarded by a series of fixed percentage points. For example:

	% increase
Unsatisfactory	0
Satisfactory	2
Above average	3½
Excellent	5

- A lump sum payment which is not consolidated into the employee's salary.

Appraisals can benefit both employers and employees. They can improve employees' job performance and suitability for promotion while at the same time helping to use labour more effectively. In addition they can improve communications and the quality of working life and make employees feel that they are valued by the organisation.

The following will help to ensure that appraisals are both effective and successful:

- Appraisals need the commitment and support of all levels of management.

- Managers and trade union representatives should be consulted before appraisals are introduced.

- Appraisals should not be seen in isolation but should be closely linked with policies and practices in other areas such as manpower planning, training and pay.

- Those responsible for appraisals should receive adequate training to enable them to make objective assessments and to give them confidence in carrying out effective appraisal interviews.

- The purpose of appraisals and how the system operates should be explained to those who are being appraised.

- Paper work should be kept to a minimum and appraisal forms should be simply and clearly designed.

- Appraisal systems should be reviewed periodically to ensure that they meet changing needs.

The introduction of a formal appraisal system does not remove managers' responsibilities for reviewing performance on a day to day basis. Employees should therefore be made aware of their strengths and weaknesses on a regular basis so that there are no surprises for them when they are formally appraised at the end of the reporting period.

It is important that appraisal systems are designed to suit the particular needs and size of the organisation. ACAS can help organisations to introduce or review appraisal systems and can be contacted at the appropriate regional office (addresses and telephone numbers are at the back of this booklet).

Appraisal – The legal considerations

Employers who recognise trade unions are required (if requested by the union) to disclose information[3] for the purposes of collective bargaining. In these circumstances, particularly where merit pay schemes are in operation, they may be requested to explain how appraisal systems operate and to describe the criteria against which employees are rated.

The Data Protection Act[4] gives individual employees a legal right of access to personal data (such as appraisal details) held about them on computers. 'Personal data' includes not just factual information but also opinions expressed about employees. Therefore employees could have access to opinions recorded about their performance or attitude at an appraisal. However, any indication of intentions, such as an intention to promote, is outside the scope of the Act. Manual personnel records are not covered by the legislation.

Under the Race Relations and Sex Discrimination Acts employees who feel they have been refused promotion or access to training on grounds of their race or sex have the right to make a complaint to an industrial tribunal. In such cases appraisal forms and procedures may be used by employees to support their complaints. It is important therefore for employers to regularly monitor their appraisal systems and promotions policies to ensure that criteria used to assess performance are non – discriminatory in terms of both race and sex.

The Commision for Racial Equality (CRE) recommends[5] that staff responsible for performance appraisals should be told not to discriminate on racial grounds. The Equal Opportunities Commission (EOC) recommends[6] that appraisal systems should assess actual performance in the job (which is not affected by the sex of the job holder). The EOC further advises employers to ensure that women are not rated lower than men who are performing at a comparable level.

---

[3] See ACAS Code of Practice No 2 *Disclosure of information to trade unions for collective bargaining purposes* (available from HMSO).

[4] See *The Data Protection Act 1984 (Questions and Answers on the Act)* – The Data Protection Registrar.

[5] CRE *Race relations Code of Practice*.

[6] EOC *Guidelines for Equal Opportunities Employers*.

'It is important to establish a procedure for informing employees in writing of unsatisfactory markings.'

Employees dismissed on grounds of inadequate performance and who subsequently complain of unfair dismissal sometimes indicate in their applications that they have received little or no indication of alleged poor performance while in employment. Appraisal schemes should not be used as a disciplinary mechanism to deal with poor performers but it is important to establish a procedure for informing employees in writing of unsatisfactory markings. The consequences of failure to meet the required standards should be explained to the employee and confirmed in writing. The appraisal form however is not the place to record details of verbal or written disciplinary warnings. These should be recorded separately as part of the disciplinary procedure. There should be space on the appraisal form to record unsatisfactory performance together with notes of action to be taken, both by the individual and by management, to remedy these deficiencies. The ACAS Advisory Handbook[7] on discipline gives advice on dealing with poor performance.

---

[7] See ACAS Advisory Handbook – *Discipline at work.*

Introducing appraisals
A Checklist

WHY?
WHAT ARE THE OBJECTIVES?

- [ ] Assessment of past performance and the improvement of future performance
- [ ] Assessment of future potential/ promotability
- [ ] Assessment of training and development needs
- [ ] To assist reward review

HOW OFTEN?

- [ ] Annually
- [ ] Bi-annually
- [ ] Quarterly
- [ ] Other

WHAT METHODS?

- [ ] Rating scales
- [ ] Comparisons with objectives
- [ ] Critical incidents
- [ ] Ranking
- [ ] Narrative report
- [ ] Behaviourally anchored rating scales
- [ ] Other/a mixture of the above methods

WHO IS TO BE APPRAISED?

- [ ] Managers
- [ ] Supervisors
- [ ] Scientists, technologists and technicians
- [ ] Sales and marketing
- [ ] Clerical
- [ ] Skilled
- [ ] Semi-skilled
- [ ] Unskilled
- [ ] Any other

WHO SHOULD CARRY OUT THE APPRAISALS?

- [ ] Immediate supervisor
- [ ] More senior manager
- [ ] Self assessment
- [ ] Personnel Manager
- [ ] Any other

SHOULD APPRAISALS BE 'OPEN' OR 'CLOSED'?

- [ ] 'Open'
- [ ] 'Closed'
- [ ] Partially open (ie. certain parts of the report not disclosed to the employee)

Example of an appraisal scheme for manual employees

NAME	JOB TITLE	DATE OF APPRAISAL

LENGTH OF TIME IN POST	DEPARTMENT

1 JOB DESCRIPTION (To be agreed with the employee)

2 ASSESSMENT OF PERFORMANCE (tick as appropriate)

	SUPERVISOR'S COMMENTS	A 7-8 — Well ahead of standard performance	B 5-6 — More than satisfactory, slightly above job requirements	C 3-4 — Less than satisfactory needs slight improvement	D 1-2 — Unsatisfactory. Below the standard reasonably expected
VOLUME OF WORK How does the amount of work done compare with the job requirement?		Exceptionally high output	Output is usually above average	Output is occasionally unsatisfactory	Insufficient – improvement needed
JOB KNOWLEDGE Does the employee have the knowledge to do the job properly?		Exceptionally thorough knowledge of own and related work	Good knowledge of own job and related work aspects	Lack of job knowledge sometimes hinders progress	Inadequate knowledge of own work
SAFETY AWARENESS Consider in regard to safe working practices		Highly motivated towards safety. Always insists on safe working practices	A good attitude to safety and encourages others likewise	Sometimes has to be reminded of safety precautions at work	Disregards basic safety precautions

	SUPERVISOR'S COMMENTS	A	B	C	D
DEPEND-ABILITY How well does the employee follow procedures?		Always thoroughly reliable	Little supervision required	Requires more frequent checks than normal	Requires constant supervision
TEAMWORK How well does the employee work with others to accomplish the goals of the job and work group?		Works extremely well with others and responds enthusiastically to new challenges	Co-operative and flexible	Usually gets along reasonably well but occasionally unhelpful	Unco-operative, resists change
ATTENDANCE & PUNCTUALITY What is the employee's pattern of absence and punctuality?		Exceptionally punctual. Rarely absent	Attendance levels are acceptable and is rarely late	Absence and/or lateness levels are higher than average	Frequently late and/or absent
WORK PLANNING Consider employee's success in planning own work		Displays excellent planning ability	Organises work well	Needs to improve some aspects of work planning	Does not plan effectively
COMMUNI-CATION How effective is the employee at verbal and written communication?		Exceptionally effective in all written and verbal communication	Usually a good communicator	Some difficulties with written and/or verbal communication	Does not communicate effectively
OVERALL MARKING		Well ahead of standard performance	More than satisfactory. Slightly above job requirements	Less than satisfactory. Needs slight improvement	Unsatisfactory. Below the standard reasonably expected

GENERAL COMMENTS BY SUPERVISOR ON THIS ASSESSMENT

Signed ....

COMMENTS BY SUPERVISOR'S MANAGER

Signed ....

ACTION PLAN AGREED TO DEVELOP EMPLOYEE AND/OR THE JOB

Include any training or counselling requirements

CAREER DEVELOPMENT – Possible steps in career development

AGREED ACTION PLAN – JOB AND DEVELOPMENT OBJECTIVES – Time Scale

Example of a rating
scales scheme

NAME	JOB TITLE	DATE OF APPRAISAL

LENGTH OF TIME IN POST	DEPARTMENT

OVERALL PERFORMANCE

The objectives of this section are to provide the employee with clear feedback about overall performance.

Check the box below which best summarises the employee's overall performance against work expectations. Your rating should consider: how well work assignments were achieved; how the employee went about achieving them; their difficulty; and what other results were achieved apart from planned assignments. When possible, take into consideration your experience with other employees in similar jobs and along the same factors. The rating scale includes three ranges of acceptable and one level of unacceptable performance, defined as follows:

Exceeded Expectations   Achievements consistently exceeded objectives or requirements.   ☐

Achieved Expectations   Achievements consistently met the majority of objectives or requirements. In some areas, accomplishments may have exceeded work expectations whereas in others, they may occasionally have slightly fallen short; however, the overall performance is acceptable for accomplishing objectives or requirements.   ☐

Below Expectations   Achievements frequently did not meet several of the objectives or requirements. With improvements in designated areas of the development plan, this employee should perform at a more satisfactory achievement level.   ☐

Not Acceptable   Achievements consistently fell below objectives or requirements. Counselling and/or disciplinary action should be considered unless improvement is shown.   ☐

Job description (to be agreed with the employee)

Outline the main duties of the job and estimate the percentage of time which is taken up with each duty.

Buyer — Department store

Decide on range, type, quantity and quality of merchandise to be bought. Visit trade fairs, shows etc and interview representatives at store. (40%)

Place orders with appropriate suppliers endeavouring to obtain the most advantageous terms possible. (20%)

Check that goods delivered are satisfactory and comply with orders. (10%)

Decide on economic selling price for goods. (10%)

Monitor sales in store to determine repeat orders, special sales promotions, or price reductions. (10%)

Keep appropriate records and prepare reports as required, e.g. sales forecasts, budget estimates. (10%)

Performance Factors

This section enables you to describe in more detail how the employee goes about achieving the results of the job by diagnosing relative strengths and weaknesses along different performance factors. For each factor use the COMMENT space to give specific examples, typical of this employee's performance, which illustrate the effectiveness rating given and any factors which have influenced performance.

PERFORMANCE FACTOR AND DEFINITIONS	COMMENTS
1 **VOLUME OF WORK:** Volume of work done compared with the job requirement.	
2 **QUALITY OF WORK:** Accuracy and presentation of work.	
3 **KNOWLEDGE OF JOB:** Understanding job procedures, equipment and methods, responsibilities and scope of duties.	

PERFORMANCE FACTOR AND DEFINITIONS	COMMENTS
4 DEPENDABILITY: The degree to which this person can be counted upon to do what is required in carrying out assigned tasks and to meet deadlines. Include comments on attendance and punctuality.	
5 INNOVATION: The degree to which methods and policies are continuously examined and suggestions made for new and better ones.	
6 STAFF DEVELOPMENT: Consideration for subordinates shown; their performance planned, monitored, appraised and developed.	
7 COMMUNICATION: Ability to convey verbal and/or written information.	
8 TEAMWORK: Work relationships established with fellow employees within and outside immediate work group.	

EFFECTIVENESS RATING SUMMARY

Performance Factor	High	Medium	Low	Not acceptable
1 Volume of work				
2 Quality of work				
3 Knowledge of job				
4 Dependability				
5 Innovation				
6 Staff development				
7 Communication				
8 Teamwork				

Overall marking			
Exceeded expectations	Achieved expectations	Below expectations	Not acceptable

Overall comments

Comments by senior manager

Work Improvement Plan

This section enables you to construct a work improvement plan for the performance factors on which improvement is needed.

Performance Factor	Specific recommendations for improving employee's current job performance

Employee's comments _____

_____

_____

_____

_____

_____

_____

_____

This appraisal has been reviewed and discussed with the employee:

Employee _____ Date _____

Manager _____ Date _____

Countersigning manager _____ Date _____

APPENDIX 5

Example of a comparison

with objectives scheme

NAME	JOB TITLE	DATE OF APPRAISAL
TIME IN PRESENT POST	DEPARTMENT	

1 JOB DESCRIPTION (To be agreed with the employee)

2 OBJECTIVES FOR REVIEW PERIOD
Include any special tasks, personal training and development

3 PROGRESS TOWARDS ACHIEVEMENT OF OBJECTIVES AND FACTORS INFLUENCING RESULTS

4 OTHER ACHIEVEMENTS

5 WERE THERE ANY OBSTACLES TO THE ACHIEVEMENT OF AGREED OBJECTIVES?

6 WHAT STEPS CAN BE TAKEN TO OVERCOME THESE OBSTACLES?

7 TRAINING, DEVELOPMENT, EDUCATION
Undertaken during review period

Planned for period to next review

8 SUMMARY OF OBJECTIVES FOR NEXT ANNUAL REVIEW PERIOD

OVERALL PERFORMANCE RATING

General performance	Overall rating
	1 Achievements outstanding ☐
	2 Achievements exceeded the requirements of the job ☐
	3 Some aspects of achievement below requirements ☐
	4 Performance unacceptable at this level ☐

COMMENTS OF REVIEWER

Signature _____ Date _____

COMMENTS OF COUNTERSIGNING MANAGER

Signature _____ Date _____

COMMENTS OF EMPLOYEE

Signature _____ Date _____

Assessment of potential

NAME	JOB TITLE	DATE OF APPRAISAL
TIME IN PRESENT POST	DEPARTMENT	

SECTION A   Assessment of potential

☐ Not fitted at present for further promotion

☐ Not fitted at present but likely to become fitted within the next two years.

☐ Fitted for promotion.

SECTION B   Employee's aspirations
Describe employee's career aspirations, noting relevant details about interests, mobility, previous experience etc.

SECTION C   Job experience
Does the employee display abilities which may make him/her a suitable candidate for a job in the same grade but in a different discipline?

YES   NO   If 'yes' list job(s) identified

☐ ☐   ....

          ....

          ....

SECTION D Training

Would further training or other development action
be appropriate

Yes   No

☐   ☐

If 'yes' list forms of training recommended.

....

....   Reporting
                                                                                    Manager
....   Signed ....

SECTION E Countersigning manager's comments

Confirm whether the employee has/has not demonstrated suitability for promotion.
Explain any areas of disagreement with the reporting manager's assessment.

Signed ....

SECTION F Employee's comments on assessment of potential

Signed ....

Self appraisal

Name ....

Department ....

Date of Appraisal ....

Your next Appraisal Meeting will take place on:

Date   Time   Place

Purpose of the Appraisal Meeting To enable you to discuss, with your manager, your job performance and your future. The discussion should aim at a clearer understanding of:

(a) The main scope and purpose of your job

(b) Agreement on your objectives and tasks

(c) Standards or targets for measuring your performance.

(d) Your training and future prospects

You can prepare for the meeting and discussion by completing this form.

You may show this form to your manager. This will give him or her time to consider your problems and suggestions. If you do so, it will not be copied or filed without your permission.

If you prefer, you can use this form for your own guidance only, and not show it to anyone.

You will be given the opportunity to read the appraisal form prepared by your manager; you will be able to add your comments, and sign the appraisal form.

Bring to the appraisal meeting – your current job description.
                                – your current action plan.

SELF APPRAISAL

NAME

1 (Circle appropriate answers, and comment below)

(a) Do you have an up-to-date job description?   Yes   No

(b) Do you have an up-to-date action plan?   Yes   No

(c) Do you understand all the requirements of your job?   Yes   No

(d) Do you have regular opportunities to discuss your
    work, and action plans?   Yes   No

(e) Have you carried out the improvements agreed with your
    manager which were made at the last appropriate meeting?   Yes   No

2 What have you accomplished, over and above the minimum requirements of your
job description, in the period under review (consider the early part of the period
as well as more recent events). Have you made any innovations?

3 List any difficulties you have in carrying out your work. Were there any
obstacles outside your own control which prevented you from performing
effectively.

4 What parts of your job, do you:

(a) do best?

(b) do less well?

(c) have difficulty with?

(d) fail to enjoy?

---

5 Have you any skills, aptitudes, or knowledge not fully utilised in your job? If so, what are they and how could they be used?

---

6 Can you suggest training which would help to improve your performance or development?

---

7 Additional remarks, notes, questions, or suggestions.

Fletcher, Clive and **Williams,** Richard
Performance and appraisal and career development
Hutchinson 1985

Incomes Data Services
Performance appraisal of manual workers
IDS Study, no 390 July 1987, whole issue

Incomes Data Services and **Institute of Personnel Management**
The merit factor – rewarding individual performance
IDS Top Pay Unit June 1985

Lawson, Ian
Appraisal and appraisal interviewing. New ed.
Industrial Society 1987 (Notes for managers)

Long, Phil
Performance appraisal revisited
Institute of Personnel Management 1986

Maddux, Robert B
Effective performance appraisals
Kogan Page 1988

Pratt, Kenneth
Effective staff appraisal – a practical guide
Van Nostrand Reinhold (UK) Co Ltd 1985

Stewart, Valerie and **Stewart,** Andrew
Practical performance appraisal: designing, installing and maintaining performance appraisal systems
Gower Press 1978

This is ACAS

Using ACAS in Industrial Disputes

The ACAS Role in Conciliation,
Arbitration and Mediation

Individual Employment Rights –
ACAS conciliation between
Individuals and Employers

Conciliation between Individuals and
Employers

Improving Industrial Relations –
A Joint Responsibility

WRU Information Leaflet

Summary of publications (a listing of
WRU and other titles regularly
updated)

Meeting the challenge of change
(WRU guidelines for the successful
implementation of change in
organisations)

Meeting the challenge of change
(Summaries of WRU case-studies)

Industrial Relations Handbook
(HMSO £5)

Advisory Handbooks
Employing People – a handbook for
small firms

Discipline at work

Advisory Booklets
1 Job evaluation
2 Introduction to payment systems
3 Personnel records
4 Labour turnover
5 Absence
6 Recruitment and selection
7 Induction of new employees
8 Workplace communications
9 The company handbook
10 Employment policies
11 Employee appraisal

Discussion Papers
1 Developments in harmonisation
2 Collective bargaining in Britain:
its extent and level

Occasional Papers
24 Quality circles in perspective
27 Effective and satisfactory work
systems
31 Managing stress in organisational
change
34 New office technology
35 The integrated payment system in
practice
36 Job evaluation in transition
37 Redundancy arrangements
38 Employee commitment

WRU Bibliographies
5 Group working
15 Work Stress
27 New Technology: Robotics and
automated manufacture
50 Management of change

Codes of Practice
1 Disciplinary practice and
procedures in employment
2 Disclosure of information to trade
unions for collective bargaining
purposes
3 Time off for trade union duties and
activities (Codes of Practice are
available from HMSO)

Annual Reports
Available on request.